How to Play

Harmonica for

Beginners

A Step-By-Step Guide on

How to Play Harmonica

as A Complete Beginner

(Including Sample Songs

to Get You Started)

Introduction

In the last couple of decades, the harmonica has become one of the world's most popular and flexible instruments. This unique small instrument that is part of the wind family makes a beautiful sound and unique melodies. Its versatility and distinctive range of tones blend well with an extensive range of musical genres from jazz to classical music and rock and roll.

If you're looking for a new musical instrument to learn how to play, then the harmonica should be your go-to instrument. If it is not the easiest, it is for sure one of the direct and straightforward musical instruments even a total novice can learn to play.

This guide will give you handy hacks that'll help you master the skill of playing the harmonica. Among other things, you will learn:

- ✓ *What a harmonica is and how it works*

- ✓ *Different types of harmonicas*

- ✓ *Playing techniques and tips on positioning your mouth and hand when playing the harmonica.*

✓ *Easy to follow instructions on how to play the harmonica*

✓ *The skill of bending your notes as you inhale and exhale, along with proper breathing techniques.*

✓ *How to read and understand music notes and symbols.*

✓ *Maintenance and preventive measures to use to take care of your harmonica*

✓ *Samples of easy songs you can play and practice with as you work towards mastering the harmonica*

Let us get started:

PS: I'd like your feedback. If you are happy with this book, please leave a review on Amazon.

Please leave a review for this book on Amazon by visiting the page below:

https://amzn.to/2VMR5qr

Table of Contents

Chapter 1: The Harmonica and Its History

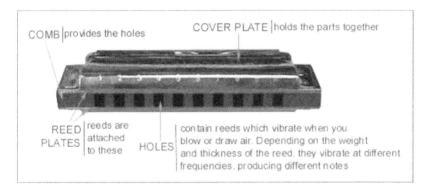

The harmonica —also called the **French harp** or **mouth organ**— is a musical instrument that is part of the wind family. You use your mouth to play the instrument with the tongue and lip helping direct air into or out of the holes along the harmonica's mouthpiece. The reed then alternatively blocks and unblocks the air passage to produce sound.

The most common harmonica is the Richter-tuned diatonic harmonica that has ten holes and twenty reeds. It is often called the **blues harp**.

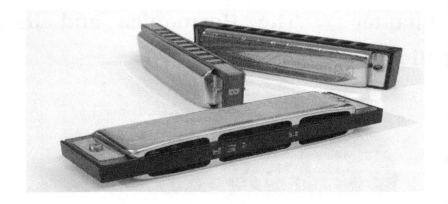

A Richter-tuned harmonica

History of the Harmonica

The harmonica was first developed from the "sheng," an ancient Chinese instrument consisting of vertical bamboo pipes mounted onto a mouthpiece through which you blow into to produce musical sounds. It dates back to 1100 BC.

Unlike the sheng, the harmonica has proved more effective since it is relatively small; it can fit perfectly into a pocket, making it very portable. Additionally, its ability to blend with different musical styles made it exceptional.

A traditional Chinese musical instrument called sheng

It was not until the early 1800s when the first harmonica was first developed in Europe, with its country of origin said to have been Germany.

Till to date, there is a lot of debate on who first invented the harmonica, some attributing it to Christian Friedrich Ludwig Buschmann, a German clockmaker, inventor, and musician. Others say it was a European named Ritcher. However, most contemporary historians state that the harmonica was invented by Christian Gottlieb Kratzenstein, a Dutch physicist and physician.

So why learn to play the Harmonic?

Research has shown that playing the harmonica can have tremendous benefits to your health.

- According to a study conducted by Madhavi Dharia Shah, this mouth organ is linked to a ton of health benefits, including boosting your lung capacity and exercising your breathing muscles. In line with Shah's book, a harmonica is a great tool that improves and strengthens your breathing. Madhavi attests that it also does wonders for respiratory issues, i.e., Asthma and bronchitis.

- Based on an article by CMUSE, a news, music, and entertainment website, the harmonica has a relaxing effect on the body and mind. As a result, it improves blood pressure levels and helps ease insomnia and attention deficit disorder. It can also help deal with depression, anxiety, and stress due to its calming effect.

- Additionally, the article also argued that you can also improve your cognitive abilities by just playing the harmonica. The French harp is very helpful to senior adults as it is said to impact the parts of their brains that control memory, hearing, and coordination.

Chapter 2: Types of Harmonicas

There are three main types of harmonics:

1: Diatonic Harmonicas

The diatonic harmonica is also known as the blues harp. This 10-hole diatonic harmonica consists of ten air passages with 12 basic keys. It contains notes of a simple major scale, and its harps are easy to learn.

This type of harmonica majorly focuses on playing a single key; the key C. A key is a root note and chord in which everything musically resolves around. Because of this, it is a great choice for you as a beginner.

However, if you're new to music, and you are probably wondering what the key C stands for, the best way is to picture a piano with only white keys instead of white and black keys.

The diatonic harmonica is often considered best for folk, country, blues, pop, and rock music.

2: *Chromatic Harmonica*

Contrary to the diatonic harmonica, the chromatic harmonica enables you to play all keys on just one instrument. It is designed to allow the musician to play each complete scale in any desired key, i.e., minor, major, pentatonic, blues, and so forth, all on one instrument.

Though there are 10, 12, 14, and 16-hole chromatic harmonicas, most are 12-hole long, with each hole containing four reeds, two chromatic notes, and two natural notes.

It isn't easy to play the harmonica, especially as a beginner. Hence, beginners should ideally start with a diatonic harmonica before stepping it up.

The chromatic harmonicas with a side sliding button are designed to be used in classical and jazz scenes.

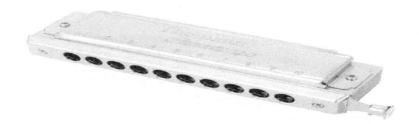

3: Tremolo Harmonica

Some people argue that this harmonica is the easiest to learn and play. This is partially true because you don't require as much technique as is the case with the diatonic or chromatic harmonica.

The tremolo harmonica only has two reeds that simultaneously vibrate when you blow and draw a note; thus, it is not as complicated as the other two main harmonicas.

That said, the tremolo has a couple of drawbacks:

- They are fairly limited.

- It doesn't allow you to play other music genres, i.e., the blues, because it involves skills such as note-bending. Thus, you will only be limited to playing very simple melodies and effects.

Like other instruments, it is always important to first understand how your instrument works before using it.

Chapter 3: Parts of a Harmonica

Regardless of the type of harmonica you are using, your harmonica is usually an assembly of five basic parts:

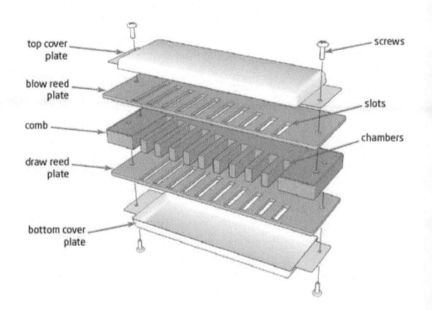

1: Comb

The harmonica is built around "the comb," a center layer usually sandwiched between reed plates. Although traditionally made of wood, over the years,' plastic and metallic combs have replaced the wooden-like combs.

It derives its name from the dividers between its channels that look like the teeth of a comb. When assembled with the reed plates, it forms air chambers with the reeds.

- A reed is ordinarily a flat-like elongated strip made of stainless steel, brass, or bronze that paves the way for air passage. When you blow air into your mouthpiece, the reed alternately blocks and unblocks its airways and vibrates to produce sound.

2: Reed plate

Reed plates are typically made from brass plates. This very square-and-flat plate has slots that house individual reeds. They are designed so that each individual reed has its own slot. The reeds are generally riveted or welded onto the reed plate, and the reed plates are then nailed or screwed onto the comb. If you look at your harmonica, you will see these screws at the edge of your harmonica.

Most harmonicas have their reed plates screwed onto the comb to prevent air blown into the holes from escaping. A harmonica usually has two reed plates, the top reed plate — for blow reeds— and the bottom —for draw reeds.

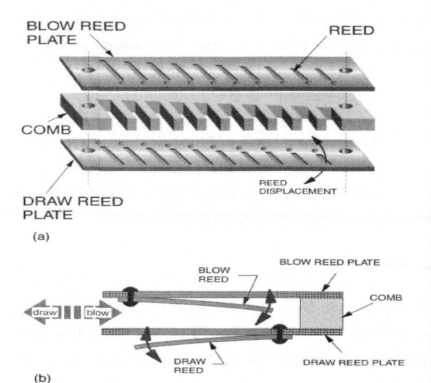

(a)

(b)

3: Cover plates

As the name suggests, these cover plates cover and shield the reed plates and the comb. Generally, cover plates are usually made of metal, though sometimes plastic and wood can also be used in their production. However, this depends on the sound quality you're trying to project since these plates determine your harmonica's tonal quality.

4: **Windsavers**

These little strips that are glued onto the reed plate lie over your harmonica reeds. Windsavers are made from plastic strips, leather, knit paper, or Teflon.

As you already know by now, the harmonica is a "windy" instrument; thus, air leakages are inevitable. For this reason, the wind savers are placed over reeds to prevent air loss through inactive reeds and help direct enough air to the appropriate reeds.

5: **Mouthpiece**

Take a look at your harmonica; you will notice holes that run through from left to right. These air chambers are situated in your mouthpiece. The mouthpiece makes playing comfortable and provides a groove when you are using a chromatic harmonica due to its slide sliding button.

Now that you know the functions of these parts, it's time to explore how they work together as a unit to produce sound.

Chapter 4: How The Harmonica Works And How To Position Your Mouth, Hand, And Tongue When Playing

Your harmonica might seem like a small instrument you can breathe into to produce melodies. However, knowing what goes inside this mysterious little box can also help you understand how to play this little instrument.

Here is a precise outlook of the inner workings of your harmonica.

➢ When you blow into your harmonica, its mouthpiece directs air from your mouth to the channels cut into the comb. These channels direct this exhaled breath to the notes. However, each note is sounded by reeds mounted on a reed plate. This exhaled air consequently pushes the blow reeds into their slots resulting in the outer wind savers opening up.

➢ On the other hand, your in-breath pulls the wind savers to seal off the blow reed slot. The air is then directed through the draw reed. This cycle causes the reeds to vibrate. In conclusion, a vibration then occurs, and the cover plate projects the sound you hear.

At this point, you are probably very eager to pick up your harmonica and start playing it. However, we also need to know how to position our hands, tongues, and mouths while playing.

How to Hold Your Harmonica With Your Hands

Did you know that by just knowing how to hold your harmonica, you are will be halfway to learning how to play?

But before you even pick your harp to take a look at it. What can you see?

If you look keenly, you'll notice a printing engraved or stamped at the top of your cover. This lets you know the name of the harmonica you are using and the side that should be on top.

After locating your cover, you will also notice that just above the holes of your harmonica, there are numbers marked on the harmonica tab, from left to right. These numbers also help you get your harmonica's right side up. So always remember that the name of your instrument and its hole numbers should always be on top.

To get you rolling, be sure to follow the steps outlined below: -

i.   Maintain an upright position, with your arms relaxed at your sides, and lift your harmonica to your chest level.

ii.   Place your harmonica between your thumb and left forefinger, as if you are about to pinch something. Make sure your thumb is parallel to your left forefinger and that your instrument's left end is resting inside your purlicue, the space between your thumb and extended forefinger.

When holding your harmonica, always position its lowest note on the left. ***How do you know which is end is your lowest note?***

The numbers embossed on your instrument will come in handy as you seek to locate the end with the lowest note. More often than not, the hole that has a number "1" above it is your lowest note. While this might not always be the case, it should be the case if you're using a regular harmonica.

iii.   After that, while still holding your harmonica, bring your right hand below your left hand and cup the harmonica to create a sealed air pocket.

While doing this, also ensure that:

- You web your fingers by bringing them close to each other to close any gaps at the back of your hands and around your harmonica

- You do not cover your mouthpiece with your hands. At all times, make sure almost half of your instrument is exposed.

iv.   Lastly, always place your right thumb at the right end of your harmonica for ease and comfort while playing.

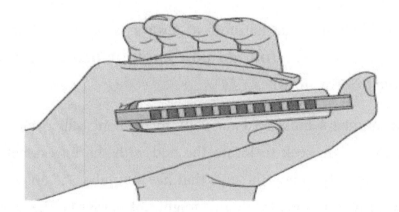

TIP: If you are just from eating or drinking something, especially a sugary beverage or something oily, always make sure you brush your teeth or rinse your mouth before you start playing.

With time, failure to do this after you have just had a meal or drink will make your harmonica have a foul taste and smell unpleasant. In addition, food residue from a meal can clog up your instrument.

How to Position Your Lips And Mouth When Playing

As you're still holding your harmonica, place it in your mouth using these steps:

- Open your mouth and use your forearms to bring your harmonica closer to your mouth.

TIP TO REMEMBER: When moving your harmonica to your mouth, don't move your head; instead, move your harmonica.

- Unfold your lips and gently close them to rest on your harp cover.

- Now try to gently blow into your harmonica and hear which sound you project. At the same time, draw to hear which sound your harmonica produces.

Now that you have tried this simple exercise, it's important to learn how to do it like a pro because most people still make many mouth positioning mistakes that cause the production of weak notes when playing.

To avoid all or some of these mistakes, here are some effective ideas you can abide by:

✓ Open your mouth as if you are yawning and slowly push your harp to the back of your mouth. When doing this, ensure that the harmonica's mouthpiece has penetrated past your front teeth. This makes sure you get full access to most of your harmonica's holes and gives you a fuller sound which is what you want.

After that, slowly tilt your harmonica such that its mouthpiece is facing downwards. This creates enough space for you to use when tongue blocking; at the same time, it makes the technique less tiring.

• Now try to jerk your tongue over your harmonica holes to the left and the right and listen to the sound your harmonica produces.

Now that you have discovered some of the coolest things about your harmonica. It is also important that you learn some tongue block techniques that you will have to use as you start your harmonica playing journey.

How to Position Your Tongue When Playing the Harmonica

There are many ways you can position your tongue while playing the harmonica but let's discuss the common techniques to get you started:

- Avoid using your tongue to block the holes of your harmonica. Alternatively, use your lower front teeth and carefully push the tongue forward such that the top of your tongue is in contact with the harmonica.

- Use the tip of your tongue when blocking a single hole. We call this technique the **pucker.** Most players adapt this single-note playing technique because it enables you to direct all the airflow from your breathe into one hole at a time. This also allows you to have smooth transitions as you move from hole to hole.

- When you want to cover more than one hole, we don't use the tip of our tongue. Instead, we use the middle part of the tongue to cover a large surface area. This technique is also used because of its efficiency when moving up and down your harmonica smoothly.

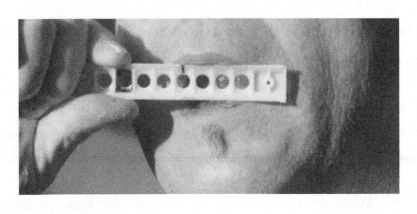

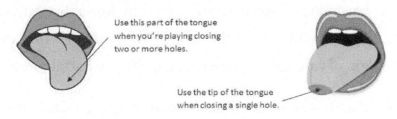

Use this part of the tongue when you're playing closing two or more holes.

Use the tip of the tongue when closing a single hole.

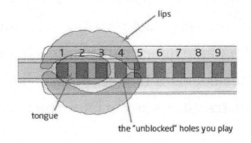

lips

tongue

the "unblocked" holes you play

I know now you are stoked to blow into these holes and hear the sound your harmonica produces. Why not? Go for it, gently blow into your harmonica and hear the sound that comes out of it. Did it sound unpleasant? If it did not, don't worry; let's work on fixing that. Remember that your instrument will not produce magical sounds because you just blew into it.

So far, we have discussed proper mouth and hand positioning when playing your harmonica. Unfortunately, all this will not make playing your harmonica easy if you don't know how to control and sustain your airflow.

Breathing plays a vital role when it comes to playing your harmonica.

At this stage, you can already tell that the sounds you are hearing coming out of your harmonica are only produced when you blow or draw on the holes. These sounds are what we refer to as **notes**.

Notes produced when you blow into your harmonica are known as **blow notes**. On the other hand, the notes produced when you suck the air out of your instrument are referred to as **draw notes**.

Later on, you shall learn that you can also change the pitch of a blow or draw using a technique we call bending. However, to produce pleasant and cool notes to the ear, it's important to learn the art of breathing without running out of breath.

Chapter 5: Proper Breathing Techniques

Without further ado, here are steps that will guide you to play blows and draws like a pro:

- Playing requires maximum concentration; therefore, the first thing you need to do is be in a relaxed state.

- Now breathe from your diaphragm by drawing air through your nose, not your mouth. As you draw in and blow out air, your stomach should be contracting and expanding. If you can't tell if you're breathing from your diaphragm, inhale and exhale while monitoring your shoulders. Should your shoulders move up and down as you breathe, you are not breathing from your diaphragm. This is key because you will control your breathing while playing and play your harmonica with ease.

- With your harmonica properly positioned in your mouth, blow and draw air from the holes situated near the middle of the comb. Inhale and exhale repeatedly until your blowing and drawing feels a bit natural.

But, how do you do this without running out of breath?

If you have tried the above exercise for more than five minutes, you will notice that you are slowly running out of breath as you progressively blow and draw. Sometimes your lips might also dry up. This is normal, especially as a beginner, because blowing and drawing is a demanding respiratory exercise. But how do we overcome this?

The best way to overcome this is by training your body, i.e., practicing this exercise every day. For example, you can try proper harmonica breathing by doing this (blowing and drawing) exercise for three minutes and add each time you pick your harp, add two minutes onto the three. Keep doing this for a whole week, and before you know it, your body will have adapted and built the endurance you need to keep you going.

<u>NOTES</u>:

- ❖ As you do this, make sure you pay attention to your posture. Maintain an upright posture by sitting up straight; also, avoid slouching your shoulders.

- ❖ Always make sure you breathe normally and always breathe from the diaphragm, not your chest. Remember that the goal is not to play harder; it's to play with ease.

❖ Before you start blowing and drawing, inhale and exhale a few times to ensure your breathing is relaxed.

Having covered all this, let's now get familiar with the musical side of things. If you blow into your harmonica, you'll produce different sounds.

To be able to play songs using your harmonica and advance your skill, you need to learn about your harmonica notes. Our main objectives are to make sure you can play on key and understand the dynamics of your harmonica.

Chapter 6: Note Layout

Before we even look at notes, your first need to understand what a key is. Musically, a key is primarily a system of related scales (minor and major), chords, and pitches in which a piece of music resolves.

This means that if you play a song in the key of C, let's say a C minor scale, the melody your harmonica produces will tend to go towards the key of C because a majority of the song will not only use notes from your C minor scale but will also use chord built from the same scale.

However, as mentioned earlier, your harmonica comes in one key, i.e., the key of G. Yours nonetheless is tuned to the key of C. Although later you will see you can play different notes and keys using your harmonica.

What Is A Scale?

In music, scales are a group of notes arranged either in ascending or descending order of pitch that a musician can build melodies and harmonies from.

However, in your harmonica, a scale forms when you take two notes that are an octave apart and concurrently add pitches in between these two notes. In addition, your diatonic harmonica has 7 notes, with scales divided into two groups.

i. Major scale

ii. Minor scale

Both scales have distinguishing features that we shall discuss shortly while discussing harmonica notes.

In addition, we also need to know about octaves, what they are, and the role they play. An octave has two notes separated from one another by 12 half steps.

To illustrate, if you've played or seen someone play the piano, you must have noticed that when you/they press the C key with your/their right thumb, you/ they will simultaneously press the next C key with their left thumb. By doing so, you or the player is trying to initiate a sequence "an octave."

Let's explore the octaves you can play on your harmonica using the note layout provided below for better understanding.

HOLE	1	2	3	4	5	6	7	8	9	10
BLOW NOTES	C	E	G	C	E	G	C	E	G	C
DRAW NOTES	D	G	B	D	F	A	B	D	F	A

- To play an octave of C using your harmonica, blow into holes 1 and 4 at the same time while blocking intermediate holes using the middle part of your tongue.

- Using your instrument, you can also play something we call the octave of E by blowing into holes 2 and 5 simultaneously or even holes 5 and 8. Don't forget to block the intermediate holes using your tongue while at it.

- Similarly, you can play two octaves of E on your C harmonica by blowing into holes 2 and 5 or holes 5 and 8 simultaneously.

Things, however, get a little bit complicated when we start talking about draw notes.

Looking at the note layout provided above, you will locate the octave of D on holes 1 and 4 or holes 4 and 8. From this example, you can already tell that the distance between the octaves is not separated by only two holes. How so? The first octave is three positions away, whereas the distance between the two is 4 positions away for the second octave.

For octave of A, the draw notes are still 4 positions away. Also, to play an octave of F, you will have to draw from holes 5 and 9, which are still 4 holes away.

Suppose you compare the blow and draw scenarios that we have witnessed above. In that case, you can tell there is some difference between the blowing octaves and the drawing ones.

Nonetheless, this should not be a problem since all you have to do is use the tongue blocking techniques we discussed earlier to get the job done.

At this moment, let's jump straight into harmonica notes.

What Is A Note?

A musical note is generally a single sound made by an instrument when played in a particular pitch. By way of illustration, using the table note layout below, you will see the draw and blow notes in your harmonic.

Hole	1	2	3	4	5	6	7	8	9	10
Blow Notes	C	E	G	C	E	G	C	E	G	C
Draw Notes	D	G	B	D	F	A	B	D	F	A

Do you remember what we said about harmonica scales?

If you do, let's use that knowledge to incorporate your harmonica notes and its scales s to get a better understanding of this:

- The C, D, E, F, G, A, B, C notes located from hole 4 to 7 make up the C major scale. And hence the reason why your instrument is in the key of C.

- If you look at the notes found at holes 1 to 4, you will notice that these notes (C, D, E, G, G, B, D, C) resemble some of the notes from hole 4 to 7. However, these low notes do not also form the C major scale. However, notes C, E, G and C make up a C major chord. If the chord concept is not clear to you yet, blow into holes 1 to 4. What do you hear? Can you hear that the notes almost make a similar sound when played together?

Similarly, from the above layout, you can tell that the blow notes appearing at holes 7 to 10 also have similar notes to those at holes 1-4. Thus, another C chord is formed at holes 7-10. Equally, the blow notes formed at holes 4 to 7 also form another C chord. On that note, I think it is safe to say that all of your harmonica blow notes resolve around the chord of C.

- By the same token, if you look at the draw notes (D, G, B, and D) that come out from holes 1-4 come from the chord G. The G chord is a very important chord when playing in the key of C.

The key and scale of the key work hand in hand to produce a good tonic sound.

Since harmonicas come only tuned in one key, harmonica players prefer to have different harmonicas so they can play in different keys. The Ritcher-tuned harmonica we shall discuss in length later is tuned to play in the key C.

If you keenly look at your harmonica, you'll notice numbers above each hole. These numbers guide you when you're playing by letting you know which hole you need to play. Each of these holes can produce a different note when you draw and blow.

If your harmonica does not have these numbers, you can mark them with the low note as your number 1 and your highest number 10. All you have to do is blow into your harmonica on one end and hear the sound created by your harmonica. If the sound is of low pitch, that end is your number 1, and if it has a high pitch, that end is your number 10.

What happens when we blow into the other holes? How do you identify the highest and the lowest note?

Let's figure it out together.

- Start by blowing into hole number 1 and follow that by drawing from the same hole.

Which note is higher? The draw or blow. If your answer was the draw note, then you're right.

- Now blow into hole number 2 and draw. You will notice that the draw note has a high pitch too.

These two instances might lead one to conclude that the draw notes are higher than blow notes. This is partly true but not accurate.

I want you to blow into hole number 10 and draw. Hopefully, you can tell the difference. Which note had the highest pitch?

> For this case, you can hear that the blow note is of a higher pitch than the draw note. Thus, the harmonica pattern switches from draw notes being higher to the blow notes, which become high pitched.

- Blow and draw into hole 3. Do the same to holes 4, 5,6, then 7.

If you are keen, you will notice that from holes 1 to 6, draw notes are higher than the blow notes. But from holes 7 through 10, the blow notes are lower than the draw notes. Hence, it is safe to say the transition happens between holes 6 and 7.

Now that you know about notes, it's time to take your skill to the next level. Have you heard of the term "do re mi fa so la ti do" used before?

If you've answered yes, you have a definite clue of what notes entail. If not, don't get worked up; you'll be up to speed within no time.

As discussed earlier, your harmonica has 10 holes, and each hole produces a note when you blow or draw. Each hole also has a different individual note it produces when you exhale and inhale. Below is a diagram that shows these notes clearly.

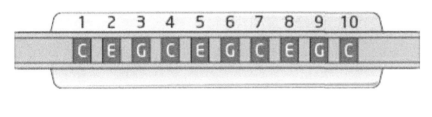

Harmonica blow notes

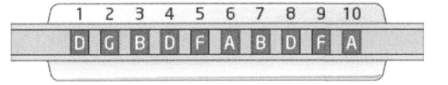

Harmonica draw notes

When played together, the blow and draw notes of your diatonic produce flowless melodies. Your harmonica contains all notes of the C major scale (C, D, E, F, G, A, B, and C). This is the first scale you will start testing your skills with, even though we fully know how these notes are interpreted.

Some notes tend to occur more than once; for instance, you can't say "play key C" because note C occurs more than four times on your harmonica. Thus, most players refer to the notes first with their number then by a blow or a draw, i.e., a player can refer to the F in hole 5 as "hole 5 draw" or to the C at hole 1 as a "1 blow" to avoid confusion.

Reading Harmonica music

Although the keys help you know which key to blow and draw from, the harmonica sheet or tablature is something you need to know. The harmonica tab precisely lets you know which hole you need to blow or draw from to produce your desired note. Some harmonica tablatures usually use up type arrows to indicate a blow note and down type of arrows to indicate draw notes.

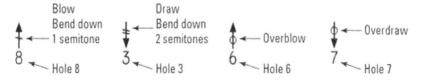

In this book, the samples of music provided will use a plain number with a positive (+) symbol before it to indicate that you need to blow into a certain hole. Alternately, a number with a minus sign (-) before it will indicate that you need to draw air from the written hole.

In some instances, you might come across harmonica tablatures with an apostrophe after them, e.g., 2'. These apostrophes usually indicate that you should bend a half step on that hole.

Example:

- -3'- this indicates you should draw bend down at hole a half a step

- -3"'- this should let you know that you need to draw bend a whole step down at hole 3

- -3"'- this denotes that you should draw bend down at hole 3 down a step and a half

The same applies when it comes down to your blow bends:

- +10'- this symbol shows that you should blow bend down a half-step in hole 10

- +10"- the double apostrophes, just like the draw bend, indicate that you bend a whole step, but it is a blow, not a draw this time.

Chapter 7: Songs To Play

At this point, it's time to test your skill and see if you are learning something.

Try:

+4-4 +5-5 +6-6 -7+7

Let's take it a notch; while using your scale provided above, try to play this

+4 -4 +5-5 +6-6 -7+7

If you are familiar with musical terms, you will notice that you just played the famous symbolic notation Do Re Mi Fa So La Ti Do.

Now try to play the sample of songs provided to test if you are on to something;

1)–Song: Oh Shenandoah

Key: C

+3   +4 +4   -4 +5 -5 -6 +6

Oh Sha-nan-doah, I long to hear you

+7 -7 -6+6   -6+6 +5 +6

a way you   roll ing riv-er

+6 -6 -6 -6

oh Sha-nan-doah

+5   +6 +5 -4 4

I long to hear you

+4-4 +5   +4+5   -6 +6

A- way, I'm bound a- way,

+4 -4   +5+4   -4 +4

Cross the wide Miss- ou- ri.

verse 2

Oh, Shenandoah, I love your daughter, Away, you rolling river Oh, Shenandoah, I love your daughter Away, I'm bound away, cross the wide Missouri.

Verse 3

Oh, Shenandoah, I'm bound to leave you, Away, you rolling river Oh, Shenandoah, I'm bound to leave you Away, I'm bound away, cross the wide Missouri.

Verse 4

Oh, Shenandoah, I long to see you, Away, you rolling river
Oh, Shenandoah, I long to see you Away, I'm bound away,
cross the wide Missouri

2)–Song: This land is your land

Musician: Woody Guthrie

Key: C

Chorus:

+3 -3 +4 +4   +4

This land is your land,

+4 +3 -3 -4 -4

 this land is my land

-1 +3 -4 -3 -3

From California,

-3 -3   +3   -3 -4 -4

to the New York Island

+3   +3 -3 -4 +4 +4

From the redwood forest,

+4 +4 +3   -3 -4 -4

to the gulf stream waters

-3 -3 -3 <-2 -1 <-2 -3 3

This land was made for you and me

+3 -3 -4 +4 +4

As I was walking

+4 +3 +3 -3 -4 -4

a ribbon of highway

-1 +3 -4 -3 -3

I- saw above me

-3 +3 -3 -4 -4

an endless skyway

+3 -3 -4 +4 +4

I saw below me

+4 +3 -3 -4 -4

a golden valley

-3 -3 -3 <-2 -1 <-2 -3 +3

This land was made for you and me

(Chorus)

+3   -3 -4 +4 + 4

 I've roamed and rambled

+4 +3 +3 -3 -4 -4

 and followed my footsteps

-1 -1   +3 -4   -3 -3

To the sparkling sands of

-3 3 -3 -4 -4

her diamond deserts

3 -3 -4 +4 +4

And all around me

+4 +3 -3 -4 -4

 a voice was sounding

-3 -3 -3 <-2 -1 <-2 -3 +3

This land was made for you and me

Chorus 3

-3 -4   +4   +4

The sun comes shining

+4 +3 -3 -4 -4

as I was strolling

-1 +3   -4   -3 -3

The wheat fields waving

 -3 -3 +3   -3 -4 -4

and the dust clouds rolling

 3 -3 -4   +4 +4

The fog was lifting

 +4   +3   -3 -4 -4

a voice come chanting

-3   -3 -3 <-2 -1 <-2 -3 +3

This land was made for you and me

(Chorus)

+3 -3 -4   +4 +4

As I was walkin'

+4 +3 -3 -4 -4

I saw a sign there

+3 -4 -3 -3

 And that sign said

+3 -3 -4 -4

no tress passin'

+3 -3 -4 +4 +4

 But on the other side

+4 +3   -3 -4 -4

it didn't say nothin!

-3 -3 -3 -3 <-2 -1 <-2 -3 +3

Now that side was made for you and me!

(Chorus)

+3 +3 +3 -3 -4 +4 +4

 In the squares of the city

+4 +4 +3 +3 +3 -3 -4 -4

In the shadow of the steeple

+3 +3 -4 -4 -3 -3

Near the relief office

+3 -3 -3 -4 -4

I see my people

+3 -3 -4   +4 +4

And some are grumblin'

+4 +3 -3 -4 -4

and some are wonderin'

-3 -3 -3   -3 <-2 -1 <-2 -3 +3

If this land's still made for you and me.

When moving from one hole to another, try to maintain the same shape to ensure you get clean and vibrant single notes.

Chapter 8: Bending Of Notes

If you have been keen enough, you can tell that your harmonica can only play up to seven different notes and 19 different pitches. Because of this, you need to learn a special technique popularly called ***bending***. Bending makes playing other notes not present on your harmonica scale easy and possible.

"Notes that are not present?"

I know that is the question you are asking yourself, but that's the truth of the matter. For instance, the diatonic harmonica has ten different notes. What does that mean?

It means your diatonic harmonica has five essential "missing" keys. So, to explore these "missing notes," bending comes in handy. To visualize this, try to whistle and after doing it the first time, alter your airflow the second time. You will notice that the sound of your whistle changes the second time after you alter your air passage. This is what happens when you are bending your draws and blows.

Changing your airflow makes your draw reeds and blow reeds at certain holes vibrate simultaneously, making the "missing" notes pop.

But is bending really necessary?

- The answer is YES because, as earlier stated, you can play some of the missing notes on your diatonic harmonica. Thus, if you are playing a melody or song that requires notes not available in your diatonic harmonica, you can produce that sound by bending your notes.

- Bend notes also add some vibrancy to your notes while playing, especially if your music resonates around blues and rock style playing.

With that said, which are these notes that are specifically missing from your C harmonica:

- C# (Db)- The notes followed by the #sign mean that the note is sharp. The b stands for a flat note. Instead of C#, some writers or books can use Db, which is the equivalent flat note.

That said, let's list the rest of the missing keys; D# (Eb), F (Gb), and A# (Bb).

NOTE: Even though you can use your harmonica to play these missing notes, it is important you also understand that you will not be able to play all of these five notes.

So, how does bending work?

Draw Bends

Generally, the notes that make up a musical scale are either one whole step or a half step apart. For example, C and C# are one-half step apart, while F and G are one whole step apart.

Bending allows you to move in half-step increments below its normal draw or blow note. For instance, in a draw bending case, if you draw from hole 4, which its drawing note is (D), you will produce a note below D which is C#.

In essence, draw bends allow you to play one-half step notes below the ordinary draw notes. Draw bending will allow you only to draw bends from holes 1-4 and 6 on your harmonica.

On hole 3, you will be able to draw bend only three notes below the hole's normal draw note B.

From note B, you can draw bend and move to A#, A, and G#.

However, on holes 1 and 6, you will be able to draw bend only a half-step below your normal draw note.

The diagram below will help you visualize the complete section of notes that you can play using draw bends to achieve these half step increments.

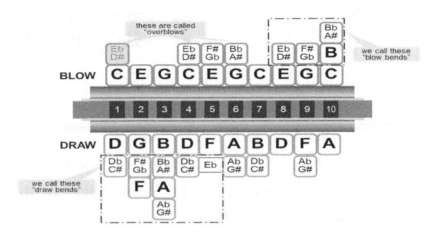

How To Draw Bend Notes Using Your Harmonica

To bend your draws, you need to control the airflow going through your harmonica's holes by moving your tongue and throat muscles as you inhale.

For a start, we shall bend the note on hole 1:

- Using the pucker embouchure discussed earlier, draw the note from your harmonica's hole 1. You can also use the tongue blocking technique if you find it easy to use. For now, let's use the pucker embouchure technique.

58

- While inhaling, try to expand the opening of your throat as you slowly lower your tongue towards the base of your mouth. If you get this combination right, you will be on the right track to draw bending notes like a pro.

TIP: As you are draw bending, don't try to inhale and strain your airflow; always make sure you maintain a normal air draw-in because when you draw in harder than you can handle, the draw bending note will be hard to enact.

- During the process of lowering your tongue, you will notice that the pitch of your note is changing to a lower tone. Thus, if you have correctly followed the steps outlined above, the note you produce should be a C#.

- Repeat this process of raising and lowering your tongue outlined from steps 1-3 as many times as possible until you can comfortably alternate from the note D to the draw bend note (C#).

TIP: Don't throw in the towel if you struggle with this draw bending technique. Instead, do this:

- Cover all your harmonica holes except hole 1 with masking tape and apply the same tape to your harmonicas' sides opposite the holes. This makes sure you focus on your bending technique instead of worrying about messing up and playing another note.

As we finalize our discussion on draw bending, keep in mind that holes 2 and 3 can allow you to draw bend notes three-half steps below their regular harmonica notes. You can achieve this by adjusting your throat muscles and controlling the depth you lower your tongue in your mouth. Generally, the more you lower your tongue, the lower the pitch is of the note you produce.

For example, if you want to play a half step below hole 2, you need to lower the position of your tongue to about a half as it can possibly go inside your mouth. Draw bending is not an easy skill, but if you follow these instructions to the letter, you will be bending your draws in no time.

Blow Bends

Blow bends allow you to bend your blow notes three-half steps below your regular blow note. These notes, however, work on holes 8, 9, and 10. The notes you can bend by bending your blows are D, F#, A#, and B.

How To Effectively Bend Blows

Like in the previous case, blow bends work the same way as the draw bends: if you change the position of your tongue and control your throat muscles when blowing, it will alter the airflow coming from your mouth. This, in turn, changes the sound of your note.

Although both techniques work similarly, there is a difference because we lower our tongue during draw bending, which is not the case when we are bending our blows. When blow bending, you raise your tongue upward to alter your airflow and tighten your throat muscles as if you are closing off the air pathway. This concept makes blow bending considerably harder compared to draw bending.

To start bending your draws, we shall start draw bending with hole 8 by draw bending note D TO D#.

- As usual, we shall use the pucker technique (single-note embouchure) to blow your notes. Again, you can use the tongue blocking method, but use the single-note embouchure for easiness.

- Exhale and as air flows out of your mouth, move your tongue upward towards your palate. This should enable you to change from D to D#.

61

While blow bending, you will notice that your throat constricts a bit. This is normal.

TIP: You can pull your jaw in toward your neck if you are having a challenge raising your tongue. It makes the process easier and smooth.

- Repeat steps 1 and 2 by alternating consistently between note D and bend note D#.

Let's try blow bending using hole number 10 this time. Blow into it and, at the same time, raise your tongue to blow bend the note. Listen to the points where you can hear three different notes. The three different notes you can hear start with the main note of the hole, which is C, then lowers to B, and finally, it lowers to an A#. If you can't tell the difference, keep practicing, and you will be able to alternate among these notes.

All you have to do is ensure you control the height of your tongue in your mouth. Progressively you will find yourself overbending though this can take years of practice to achieve. By overbending, you will be able to sound more notes on a higher pitch than most of the ordinary draw and blow notes of certain holes on your harp.

Chapter 9: Harmonica Positions

Although we have deeply discussed the impact bending has on your harmonica, there's no doubt that the instrument also comes tuned solely to play in one key, i.e., the key of C. In your case, your harp is tuned to the key of C. What happens in a situation where you want to play a melody in the key of G or F?

In such a circumstance, harmonica positions come in and become useful to you as a player.

What Are Harmonica Positions?

Harmonica positions enable you to play different keys on your C harmonica. To expound:

The C note on your C harmonica is the lowest note, which, as earlier discussed, is a blow note located on hole 1. The C note is a central pitch. Thus, the conclusion is that your harmonica is tuned in C major.

Let's consider a new type of harmonica like the one shown below:

Hole	1	2	3	4	5	6	7	8	9	10
Blow	G	C	E	G	C	E	G	C	E	G
Draw	B	D	G	B	D	F	A	B	D	F

Looking at the picture above, you will notice that the C note initially on hole 1 is now on hole 2. Does this mean the harmonica is tuned in the key of G now that the lowest note is a G note?

Not really, the above harmonica is still in the key of C, and the scale is in C major despite the G note at the start, hence the conclusion that you can play your single key harmonica in different keys.

Why don't we just bend these notes? Why is harmonica positioning that important?

For illustration:

You can use different keys to play different scales when playing a keyboard. But this only ensures you play each key solely on one particular note.

This is not the case with your harmonica, even though it is just like the piano, you can only produce a specific note with your harmonica when you blow or draw from a specific hole. For instance, if you blow into hole 4, you will play a C note.

Similarly, if you decide to draw from hole 2, it will produce a G note. However, this will be a problem if you're using an F harmonica —since all the notes on the F harmonica are different from your C harmonica. What should you do in such a situation?

For such an instance, you will have to play your harmonica in the cross harp position (2nd position) to play any of the C scales. We shall discuss this in greater detail later:

- Secondarily, even if it is possible to raise or lower your pitch by bending your notes using your diatonic harmonica, remember that this standard drawing bending technique sometimes makes it move smoothly from one note to another. Hence, to play fluently and smoothly and move from one draw bend to another blow bend draw bend, you will need to use a harmonica position.

Now let's look at these harmonica positions:

Types of harmonica positions

There are more than five harmonica positions, but most are not frequently used. For this reason, we shall only discuss the important positions you should know of to get started.

1st position (or the "straight harp")

The straight harp or 1st position involves playing your harmonica in the same key your harmonica came in. So, in your case, what this means is when you are playing your harmonica, you will be playing in the key C. This position is ideal for playing simple melodies and folk music. To give a practical example, play this major scale: +4-4 +5-5 +6-6 -7+7.

2nd position (or the cross harp)

Although the straight harp is still used, the cross harp is more popular among harmonica players because you can play, for instance, a key G on a C harmonica.

The 2nd position in your harmonica starts from hole 2 as a draw to hole 6-blow. To be able to play the key of G in the 2nd position using your harmonica count up to 7 semitones (or move perfect fifth up), i.e., from note C, D, E, F to G. Such that you start and finish all your scales on the note of G and play them using the same chord. (Draw notes from holes 1, 2, 3, and 4, for instance, make up a G chord)

TIP: A chord forms when you play two or three notes concurrently.

The benefit of playing your harmonica in the second position is that it allows you to play your high bendable notes on a much lower scale, making playing easy.

NOTE THAT; a position is not a scale. A position is the hole you will start playing on, which gives you access to the next different key.

3rd position (or the slant harp)

The third position is not as commonly used as the 1st and 2nd positions. The third positioning lets you play a tone below your initial tune key. So, in your case, your C harmonica will be playing in the key of D when playing in 3rd position.

The fourth position is used to play in the key of A when using your C harmonica to produce minor music. However, it is mainly disregarded since it makes playing keys in tune challenging and difficult.

Harmonicas have more than 5 positions, but you might never use or need harmonica positions beyond the fifth one.

At this point, I want you to give yourself a big round of applause. You now know more than 95% of the harmonica music theory.

Chord

As you already know, a chord is what we hear when three or more notes are sounded together simultaneously. Just like any other instrument, your harmonica can play chords too. Unlike keys, notes, and pitches, chords are played in the company of other instruments because you can't play chords one after another as we do with musical keys.

For instance, in a piano, piano players use chords in between their instruments' melodies to tell a song's story or, in some cases, to "uplift" and change the song's cadence. The same applies to guitar players in that they play solos over their guitar chords.

Your harmonica has different types of chords, as earlier discussed. However, as much as chords produce pleasant and harmonious sounds if wrongly placed, can be foreboding and jarring. The purpose of this statement is not to discourage you because we shall shortly make sure you get it right from the jump. Generally speaking, based on the diversity of your harp notes, harmonicas come in a diversity of different chords.

That notwithstanding, we shall discuss the most common popular chords you can play using your harmonica.

Types of chords:

a) **Major chords:** Most major chords sound "bright" or —for lack of a better term— rather lifting and pleasant. Examples of major chords in your harmonica are on your C major and G major scale. The C major chord consists of blow notes from holes 1-2-3 or 4-5-6 and 7-8-9 simultaneously. Draw notes coming from holes 1-2-3 and 1-2-3-4 make up the G major chord.

b) **Minor chords-** Minor chords sound somehow menacing and dark. An example of a minor chord is the D minor chord sounded when you draw from holes 4-5-6 and 8-9-10 simultaneously. The B minor flat-five is another minor chord you can play using your C harmonica. This minor chord is unique because it combines the qualities of a minor and the seventh chord discussed below. The B minor flat is sounded when you play the draw notes from holes 3-4-5-6 simultaneously or play at the same time the draw notes from holes 7-8-9-10.

c) **Seventh chord**: The last is the seventh chord, which, when you blow or draw from your notes, sounds somehow- as if the chords are not in "harmony."

Somewhat in the lines of neither being dark nor bright. Dissonant can be used to describe the sound heard from a seventh chord. A G seven is a perfect example chord that you can play in your C harmonica. When played simultaneously, draw notes from holes 2, 3, 4, and 5 make up a G7 chord.

Blow Chords

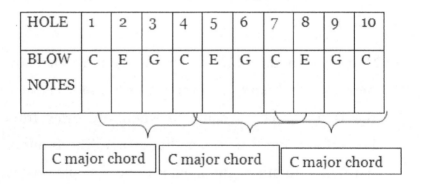

HOLE	1	2	3	4	5	6	7	8	9	10
BLOW NOTES	C	E	G	C	E	G	C	E	G	C

C major chord   C major chord   C major chord

Draw Chords

HOLE	1	2	3	4	5	6	7	8	9	10
DRAW NOTES	D	G	B	D	F	A	B	D	F	A

G7 (Seventh) chord — B minor seven flat-five

G major chord — D minor chord — D minor chord

It is now time to learn how you can position your mouth to play these chords:

- You will need to use the same mouth and hand positioning we discussed earlier to play these chords.

- The only thing you need to change is your tongue positioning. Move your tongue away from the harp's holes and let it rest at the bottom of your mouth.

- Now move your harmonica towards the right side while maintaining your lips and hands position. Note that the only thing you need to shift is your harmonica.

- After doing this, place the right holes on your mouth such that holes 1,2, and 3 align with the area your lips cover.

- Right away, blow into holes 1,2, and 3 simultaneously by exhaling from your diaphragm. By following this drill, you just sounded the C major chord. If the sound that came out sounded the same from the three holes, then you did it right; if not, repeat the process again and again! until you get it right.

Now try the above process but alternate the holes you were initially playing with by using these new holes. For instance, you can inhale from holes 1-2-3 to sound the G major chord. Try playing the G7 CHORD and D minor chord also. This can be challenging if you are not familiar with this, especially in your case since you might not know if you are playing it right.

Therefore, it is better to start with the C major chord, which is easier by following the steps outlined above. The C minor chord should sound bright and resolve around the C note.

Sample Harmonica Songs to Get You Started:

Given everything we've discussed, you are ready to try out the skills acquired to play the following set of new songs that incorporate chords:

Song 1: Long, Long, Long

By: The Beatles

-8 -8 -8   -6

IT WON'T BE LONG

-6 -8 -6 -8 -6 -8

YEH, YEH, YEH, YEH, YEH, YEH

-8 -8 -8 -8 -6

 IT WON'T BE LONG

-6 -8 -6 -8 -6 -8

YEH, YEH, YEH, YEH, YEH

-8 -8 -8 -6 -6

T WON'T BE LONG

73

-6 -8

 YEH, YEH

-6 -6 -6 -6 -6 +6

TILL I BE-LONG TO YOU

+7 -7 +6 -6 -7 -6 +5 -5 +6

EV-'RY-NIGHT WHEN EV-'RY-BOD-Y HAS FUN

7 -7 +6 -6 -7 -6 5 -5 +6

HERE AM I SIT-TING ALL ON MY OWN

Chorus:

-4 +5   +6 +6 +6 +6 -6 +6

 SINCE YOU LEFT ME I'M SO A-LONE

+6+5   +6 +6

NOW YOU'RE COM-ING

+6 -6 +6 +5 +4

YOU'RE COM-ING ON HOME

-5 -5 -5 -5 -4 5 -4 + 5 -4

I'LL BE GOOD LIKE I KNOW- I SHOULD

+7 +7 -6 +7 -6

YOU'RE COM-ING HOME

+8 -8 +7 -8 +6

YOU'RE COM-ING HOME

Song 2: The Long and Winding Road

Artist: The Beatles

Key- Bm

-7 +7 -7 +6 +5 -6

the long and wind-ing road

-6 +6 -6 -7 -6

that leads to your door

-6 -7 + 7 +6 5 -6

will nev-er dis-ap-pear

-5 -5 -5 +6 -6 6

i've seen that road be-fore

-6 -7 + 7 +6 +5 -6

it al-ways leads me here

-6 -6 -7 +7 +7

lead me to your door

+7 + 7 + 7 + 7 -8 +7 -6

man-y times i've been a-lone

+4 +5 +6 +4 +5 +6

and man-y times i've cried

+7 +7 +7 -6 -8 +7 -6

an-y-way you'll nev-er know

-5 5 +6 +4 +5 +6

the man-y ways i've tried

6 7 -7 6 5 -6

but still they lead me back

-6 +5 +6 -6 -7 -6

to the long wind-ing road

-6 -7 +7 +6 +5 -6

you left me stand-ing here

-5 -5 -5   + 6 -6 +6

a long,long time a-go

-6   -7 +7   +6   +5 -6

don't leave me stand-ing here

-6 -6 -7 +7 +7

lead me to your door

Song 3: Revolution

ARTIST: The Beatles

+5   +6   +6   +6

You say you want

+6 +7 -8 +9 +8 -8 +7

a rev-o-lu-tion-

+8 -8 +7 -6 -8 +7 -6

Well-- you know-

+8 -8 -8 +7 -8 +7 +6

We all want to change the world

+5 +6   +6 +6

You tell me that

+6 +7 -8 +7 +9 +8 -8 +7

it's e-vo--lu-tion-

+8 -8 +7 -6 -8 +7 -6

 Well-- you know-

+8 -8   -8 +7

We all want to

-8+ 7 -8 +7 -6 +6

 change the world--

-6 -8   +7 -8

But when you talk

+7 -8 +7 +8 +8 -8 +7 -6

about des-truc-tion--

-8   +7 -8 +7 -8 +7 +8 +8 -9

Don't you know you can count me out

+6 -6   +7 -6   +7 -6 +8 +8 -8

Don't you know it's gon-na be al-right

+8 -8   +8 -8

Al-right Al-right

1) Song: Viva La Vida

Artist: Coldplay

+8 +8 +8 +8 -9 -8

I used to rule the world.

-8 +6 -8 -8 +7 +8 +6 -6

Seas would rise when I gave the word.

+8 +8 +8 +8 +8 +8 8 -9 -8

Now in the morn-ing I sweep a-lone.

-8 +6 -8 -8 -8 +8 +7 -7 -6

Sweep the streets I used to o--w--n.

+8 +8 +8 +8 -9 -8

used to roll the dice.

-8 +6 -8 -8 6 -8 -8 +8 +7 -7-6

Feel the fear in my e-ne-my's e-y-es.

+8 +8 +8 +8 +8 -9 -8

Lis-ten as the crowd would sing.

+7+ 7 +8 -8 7 +7

'Now the old king is dead!

+7 +8 -8 +7 +7

Long live the kin-g!'

-10 -10 -10 -10 -10 +8 +9

One mi-nute I held the key.

+9 +9 +9 +7 +9 -8 +8

Next the walls were closed on me.

+6 +8 +8 +8 +8 +8

And I di-sco-vered that

+8 +8 -9 -8

my ca-stles stand.

+7 +7 8 -8 +7 +7 +8

U-pon pil-lars of salt and

-8 +7 +7 -7

pil-lars of sand.

+7 -10 -10 -10 +9 -10 +9 -8 +8 -9

I hear Je-ru-sa-lem bells a ring-ing.

+9 +9 +9 +8 +9 +8 -6 -7 +7

Ro-man Ca-val-ry choirs are sing-ing.

 -10 -10 -10 +9 -10 +9 -8 +8 -9

Be my mir-ror, my sword, and shie-ld.

+8 +9 +8 +9 +9 +8 +9 8 -6 -7 +7

My mis-sio-nar-ies in a fo-reign fie-ld.

+9 +9 +9 -9 +9 -10 -10 -10

For some rea-son I can't ex-plain. 9

+9 +9 +9 -9 +8

Once you go, there was ne-ver.

-9 +8 +8 +8 -9 -8

Ne-ver an ho-nest word.

 -9 -8 -7

That was when

+7 +8 -7 +7

I ruled the world.

Song 4: Martha My Dear

Artist; The Beatles

-8 + 7   +6

Dear Pru-dence,

+7 -6   +7 +7 -8 +7 -6 +6

won't you come out to play--

-8 + 7 +6

 Dear Pru-dence,

+7 -6   +7 +7 +7 -6 +6 +8

greet the brand new day-ha-hay-hay

+6 +7 -8 +7 +6 +7 -8 +7

The sun is up, the sky is blue

+6 +7 -8 +7 +6 + 7 -8 +7

It's beau-ti-ful and so are you

-8 +7 +6

Dear Pru-dence,

-8 -8 -8 +7 +7 + 7

won't you come out to play?

Song 5: Love Me Do

Artist: The Beatles

Key -G

Intro:

-5 5 -4 +4 +3 +3,

-5 5 -4 +4 +3 +3,

-5 5 -4 +4 +3,

3 3 -4 +4

+3 +3 +3 -4 +4

-4   -4 +5 +6

Love, love me do.

+4 -4 -4 +5 +6

You know I love you,

+4 -4 -4 +5 +6

I'll al-ways be true,

-5 +6 -5 +5 +6 +3 +3 -5 5 -4

So please- - -, love me do - - .

-5   +5 +5 -4

Whoa, love me do.

verse 2.

Love, love me do.

You know I love you,

I'll always be true,

So please, love me do.

Whoa, love me do.

-4   -4 +4 -3

Some-one to love,

+6 -5 +5 -4

Some-bod-y new.

-4   -4 +4 -3

Some-one to love,

+6   -5   +5 -4

Some-one like you.

(FILL)

+3 +3+3 +3 +3 +4 -4,

+3 +3 +3 -4

verse 3.

Love, love me do.

You know I love you,

I'll always be true,

So please, love me do.

Whoa, love me do.

verse 4.

Love, love me do.

You know I love you,

'll always be true,

So please, love me do.

Whoa, love me do.

Yeah, love me do.

Whoa, oh, love me do.

In-text citation

2021© Petaxxon Online Communication

Reference entry

https://m.e-chords.com

Chapter 10: Harmonica Care and Maintenance

Now that you are a bit familiar with your harmonica, tap it (holes down) against the palm of your hand several times. What do you see? Do you see any foreign substances and moisture coming out of it? If yes, don't panic; this is prone to happen when you play your harmonica.

As much as it is normal, it will wear out your harmonica and reduce its lifespan. Your harmonica should serve you for more than a few years before your reeds start wearing out, and you need to replace them.

However, the excess moisture you have seen, which is saliva and other foreign substances, can make you have to replace your harp with another one in less than six months. What can you do to prolong your harmonica's lifespan?

If you research ways to take care of your harmonica online or in harmonica instruction books, you will notice that most of them will tell you to soak, rinse or boil your harmonica. Other sources or players will even tell you to soak your harmonica in beer because they did that when starting up without knowing of its effects. Little did they know they were destroying their harmonica's beyond repair.

For instance, if you boil your harmonica, you will corrode your reeds and reed plates. In addition, it will gradually destroy your wind-saving valves, and your painted surfaces might also peel off as a result of boiling.

To keep your harmonica in shape, we are going to start with a few tips that you will need to follow:

- Always make sure you warm up your harmonica before you pick it up and start playing it. Why is this important?

This is key because from the tapping exercise you just did, you can attest that your harp slowly builds up moisture when you are playing it. Thus, when you warm it up, you prepare your harmonica to resist this moisture build-up and even prevent foreign substance clogging.

It is essential that you also understand that by "warming" up your harmonica, you use either a warming pad or place the instrument between your hands. You can also place your harmonica in between your arms to warm it up or even back pocket

NOTE: You should never warm your harmonica to a level that it becomes so hot, all in the name of warming it. This is because most of your harp parts are metal-made. Thus, by heating your harp, these parts can melt, damaging your instrument irreparably.

Your safety is also important since we don't want you to burn your tongue or hands when playing your harmonica. Owing to that fact, just **warm** up harmonica such that it is not cold but warm enough that you can play it and resist moisture build-up.

WARNING: On no occasion should you ever place your harmonica on or close to a radiator or heater.

- In addition, the moisture that builds up in your harmonica is bad for your harmonica. But to what extent does it affect your harmonica? In the long term, some of your harmonica plates corrode because of this moisture build-up from your saliva and external fluids. Furthermore, other contaminants that get blown into your harmonica by the mouth cause your wooden comb to swell and warp. Thus, always tap the loose saliva out of your harmonica between songs or after playing a song.

To do this, all you have to do is to hold your harmonica with its holes facing downwards and gently tap it against your palm, towel, or leg.

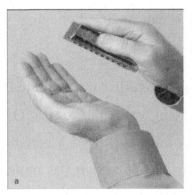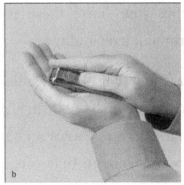

After playing, remember to dry it in the air before putting it away.

TIP: You should keep your harmonica in a preferably sunny, dry location away from children and pets.

- How you store your harmonica is something you should not overlook too. It is best if you carry it in a pouch or box. Most harmonicas come in with a pouch or box. Always place yours inside its box or pouch once you stop playing. This might seem like a non-issue, but by just placing your harmonica in its box or pouch, you protect it from hair, lint, and other foreign particles that end up clogging your harmonica. If your harmonica interest grows and you want to get other harps, you can get wallets, cases, and even wallets to carry your harmonicas.

- Another vital thing you need to do is to ensure you clean your mouth before picking up your harmonica and playing it. You can do this by rinsing your mouth with water, especially if you just ate or drank something because food residue, sugar, and other contaminants from non-water beverages slowly build up and clog your harmonica. On that same note, ensure you refrain from playing your harmonica right after brushing your teeth.

- As a general rule, never allow a second party to play your harmonica.

TIP: On top of that, avoid smoking cigarettes when playing your harmonica.

- Besides rinsing your mouth after eating sugary or thick food or after brushing your teeth, your second line of defense is playing your harmonica with clean hands. Most viruses are more often than not picked up by your hands and then transferred to your lips or eyes by rubbing into them. Likewise, germs are transferred to your harp by your hands then to your lips. For this reason, you should wash your hands to avoid getting ill and have less playing time.

Cleaning Your Harmonica

The better you take care of your harmonica, the longer your harp lasts. That's why it is important to clean your harmonica, but at the same time, how you clean the instrument is also crucial.

Most books will advise you not to wash your harmonica because it is unnecessary. This might be partially true because washing your harmonica can cause rusting of the inner parts of your harmonica. However, although this is somehow true, you need to clean your harmonica regularly and in the correct way.

Method 1

How to clean your harmonica with lukewarm water:

This exercise should be part of your washing routine if your harmonica combs are made of either alloy, plastic, or heavily sealed combs. If your harmonica's comb material is not made of any of the above materials, all you should do is take a small brush and scrub its holes.

How do you know what your harmonica comb is made of?

Easy: look at your instrument. If the comb looks like plastic, it is plastic. If it looks like an alloy, then it is made of alloy.

Let's pick up from where we left off!

- Pick up your harmonica and rinse it with lukewarm water, running water through its holes.

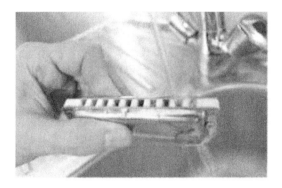

- As discussed earlier, do this for about 5 minutes and then tap it against your towel or hand. After doing that, leave it to dry by placing it in a sunny, dry location.

Method 2

Full cleaning

It is good to give your harmonica a thorough and full deep cleaning once in a while by disassembling your harmonica and cleaning its insides.

How to perform heavy cleaning on your harmonica

- Start by removing its screws with an appropriate screwdriver while holding its cover plate. Make sure that the screwdriver you are using is of the appropriate size. Once you have removed your screws, place them in a safe place where they can be traced back.

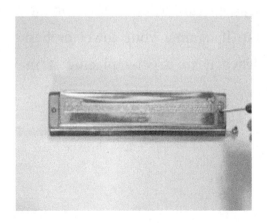

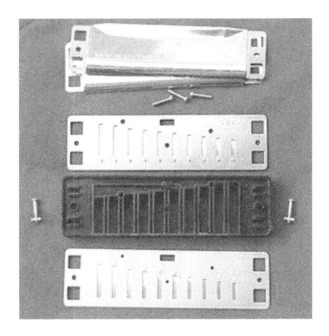

- Spray both sides of your cover plates with either isopropyl alcohol or rubbing alcohol, and then wipe the alcohol with a soft cloth.

- After removing your cover plates, slowly remove your reed plates. If they're attached to your reed plates, you can use your screwdriver to remove the screws.

TIP: Remove the screws and keep them somewhere safe using the order you used to remove them so that placing them back in the right hole can be easy.

- After that, soak your reed plates into a vinegar solution or warm water and let them soak for 30 minutes. While your reed plates are soaking up, clean your comb. If it is made of plastic, you can clean it with soap and water. You can also spray it with alcohol and use a soft brush to brush it. If your harmonica is made of wood, you should not use water or soap to clean it. In such a case, use a brush or a sharp object to dig up any gunk in your comb. If yours is made of metal, ensure you thoroughly dry the comb before reassembling.

- Now pick up your reed plates and clean them using a soft toothbrush, being careful not to scrub your harmonicas' reed plates with your toothbrush while brushing them. Ensure that you also don't brush your reed plates against their reeds. This will damage them and mess up your notes when you are playing.

TIP:

- Always ensure you brush your reed plates along your reeds, not across them.

- You can vigorously clean the other side of your reed plates since it has no reeds.

- You can use hydrogen peroxide to clean your reed plates if you have it.

- Place these parts out in the sun, away from pets, and let them dry completely. Reassemble these parts and gradually screw your screws back and evenly tighten them.

Conclusion

If you have read this book from the beginning to the end, you now have all the tools you need to create a musical journey around your harmonica. As unbelievable as it sounds, you are now past the beginner level, and thanks to the steps and tips planted in your mind by this book, you can now play the harmonica well.

In conclusion, remember to be patient with yourself; *persistent practice is the key to mastery.*

PS: I'd like your feedback. If you are happy with this book, please leave a review on Amazon.

Please leave a review for this book on Amazon by visiting the page below:

https://amzn.to/2VMR5qr

Made in the USA
Las Vegas, NV
06 May 2024

89591276R00056